# Dostoevsky's Characters in a Darwinian World:

# Gender Models in the Evolution of Political Behavior – The Impact of Rape and Genocide in post-Neolithic East Europe

## Gary Cox

*This study was published in 2001, in a relatively obscure scholarly journal, and attracted little notice. At that time it was still taboo to say that men and women are different. The author left academia soon after that, and has spent most of the past decade working in tourism in Russia and east-central Europe, keeping a hand in with academic scholarship only with an occasional invited book review. Recent events have prompted another look at this piece, and it is now presented to the general public in a less esoteric version. The scholarly original is available too (see below), with all the footnotes, bibliography, disclaimers, and forbidding, arcane jargon.*

Dostoevsky's characters sort themselves into a typology themed around charismatic dominance. His heroes and villains are tyrants and victims, and his works spin on an axis formed between those opposites. What saves it all from becoming melodrama, one thing anyway, is role reversal - Dostoevsky's tyrants tend to bow to his victims at the end, and everybody gets saved, sometimes even in the religious sense. The other thing that keeps it from cloying is that he always knocks the type askew with at least one detail that doesn't fit - the whore is a devout, Bible-reading Christian, the atheist writes articles on church governance, the rake has a penchant for self-humiliation, and so forth. As a result, characters based on melodramatic types shimmer with contradictions and fascinate us with their complexity. That's one reason why believers and nihilists alike continue to read his books with passionate excitement.

Of course there are gender elements to this dyad, as we would expect given the way gender abuse works. The victims are more often women, the tyrants more often men. The reversals of Dostoevsky's works can have both redemptive religious meanings and raunchy erotic ones. Just like real life, in fact. Another reason we keep eagerly turning pages, whether we agree with the author's ideas or not.

When I put forward the 'tyrant-victim axis' as a key to Dostoevsky, in the early 1980s, I compared his characters to a tribe of islanders, and called the author an anthropologist of sorts, giving us a key to group behavior. Charismatic dominance and the tyrant/victim dyad operate not only between individuals in groups, but between groups as they interact with each other, so this pattern, including its gender-typical elements, can motivate political systems as they develop in human societies.

This takes us into evolutionary psychology (forgive me, Fyodor Mikhailovich!), the relatively new field that investigates the origins of human behavior in our evolutionary past. It is proving possible to view changing human behavior, even cultural behavior, as a set of adaptations to changing environments, including cultural environments. Looking at Dostoevsky in Darwinian terms gets a bit funky, since Dostoevsky leaped into orthodox (and Orthodox) Christian faith as a solution to the problems posed in his works, and loathed Darwin and the whole naturalistic approach. As with any great writer, though, the characters have lives of their own, and we as readers are free to look at them any way we like.

One dimension of the Dostoevskian 'tyrant-victim' complex is the cliche that the 'Russian soul' is passive. Russian political culture stymies initiative, according to this truism; it lowers confidence in positive return, impairs one's sense of competence to act, even in everyday matters. Russian society sorts itself into a controlled mass and a distant controlling elite. Direct political action is seldom attempted; subversion of control mechanisms, often through brilliant works of literature, has been a preferred route to change.

Since 1991, western observers, expecting a middle class of empowered consumers to emerge in Russia once the invisible hand of capitalistic democracy was untied, have been dismayed by the culture's persistent bifurcation into top-heavy authority or oligarchy and a dispossessed mass. The behavior pattern resists change, although the leadup to the 2012 election is showing signs that it is finally appearing. This sort of persistent dysfunctional behavior is just the kind of pattern that an evolutionary approach can explain best.

Another version of this observation has been the assertion of "Russia's feminine soul". What is meant is, of course, that Russian society typically allows itself, even more than most, to be constrained by a hyperactive authority system that is construed as masculine. This indisputably happens - it could be called with equal justice a hyper-masculine society, after the authority system itself. The important point is that Slavic authority systems mimic patriarchal systems of personal control, and the 'tyrant/victim dyad' of Dostoevsky's work echoes this.

In a nutshell, there is an authority deficit at the center of everyday life in such cultures, with two reaction formations. What I call the 'androtypic' reaction produces an overly strong authority system which comes to dominate political life, while a 'gynotypic' reaction system allows itself to be co-opted by the political system, but finds effective ways to subvert it, often through artistic and other cultural behaviors.

You don't have to look far to find androtypic tyranny - It's cheap and widespread! What's distinctive about Russia is the cultural response of subversion through literature. So it's no insult to say the Russian soul is feminine - It gives the culture a very special identity and a unique place in human cultural evolution. Indeed, to construe the idea of a feminine soul as insulting embodies an underlying implicit sexism!

This paper contends that this trait set is a vestige of neurocultural adaptation to post-neolithic conditions. Its inception can be traced using evidence from archaeology, folklore, linguistics and ancient history, and current instances can be tracked in studies of contemporary culture and literature. The behavioral template very likely evolved in the kinship system when local politics was kinship-linked; so it is close to matters of personal identity. This line of research will take us far afield from the Dostoevskian perceptions that occasioned the study, but we will come round full circle to Dostoevsky in the end.

## Ethnographic dimensions.

Let us start with prehistoric ethnography of Eastern Europe. We need to look at four types of behavior in the ancestral Slavic period: economic/hierarchical and kinship/gender, since it turns out that these four are related. The ancestral period for Slavs lasted roughly from 500 BC to 500 AD, when the environment supported two types of agriculture: nomadic herding and settled farming. Nomadic pastoralism (herding) was a specialty of the Central Asians who may have brought proto-Indo-European language, extensive stockbreeding, and considerable plunder and rapine, to disrupt the societies of peaceful farmers of old neolithic Europe about four millenia earlier, and who kept on sweeping westward through the middle ages.

Indeed, herding societies have tended

collectively to androtypic behavior, with strong military organization This makes perfect evolutionary sense: in foraging societies men hunt. Then someone gets the bright idea of managing the hunted animal in captivity, and hunting becomes herding. Conversely, settled farmers may be said to follow a gynotyic pattern, exactly what evolutionary thinking would predict. Women gather in foraging societies; as they learn more about the foodstuffs they gather, they start planting and tending them.

The environment, and maybe the climate, motivated a "farmer/cowman" dyad in east Europe from 500 BC to 500 AD: the landscape with its rolling grasslands fading off into semi-arid regions to the southeast, and the fertile black earth, bordering them on the north and west, watered by great rivers and betimes protected by dense forest, betimes not. Of course, sedentary horticulture eventually comes to be typical of most societies, but this environment not only enabled both of these economic paradigms, but it seems to have set them up in bipolar tension, symbiotic or simply oppositional, but in any case a functional dyad.

Furthermore, this polarity seems independent of ethnicity. While proto-Slavs and proto-Balts typically took up horticulture, the nomadic herders in question were ethnically diverse: Scythians, Sarmatians, and Alans spoke languages which were Indo-European but connected to Iranian; Goths represented the Germanic branch of Indo-European, Huns spoke something Turkic, later groups (after the emergence of Slavic ethnic groups) spoke Hungarian, Turkish again (although these Turks went around the Black Sea's south side, they ended up in east Europe too), and finally Mongol.

Closer to our own age, along come the Cossacks, east Slavs whose warlike nomadism mimicked the androtypic behavior of these earlier ethnic groups. Of course they are only marginally an "ethnic group", arising as they did on the edge of east Slavic ethnicity (Russian-Ukrainian) - They were basically east Slavic peasants fleeing southwest from tsarist tyranny (or southeast from Polish aristocrats) and from edicts that would have bound them to the land as serfs. Their adoption of herding on a military model, in the same region where Scythians, Goths, and Huns had done the same a millenium earlier, supports the idea that it was the environment, together with historical developments, that conditioned this choice.

One could argue that the physical

environment, together with aspects of the cultural environment (the level of agricultural technology) set up two evolutionary niches, farmer and cowman, in a symbiotic dyad. Those niches could be occupied by various ethnic groups, realizing various incipient behavioral systems, apparently activated by the accidents of (pre-)history.

The linguistic boundary between Baltic and Slavic was porous in 500 BC, and on some topics, notably religion, the same was true of Slavic and Scythian (Indo-Iranian), as most of the pre-Christian Slavic religious terms are virtually identical with the corresponding terms in Iranian. Whatever their economic and military differences, and whatever their living arrangements, Scythians (and Sarmatians) and proto-Slavs were a religious unity, and at least to that extent a linguistic one. For practical purposes, because of conquest rape (see below) we may also consider them functionally a single breeding group. For all of these reasons, ethnic boundary lines mean something very different when we talk about this ancestral period - One may separate genetic, linguistic, and social elements of what we usually call ethnicity. The nomadic Scyth aristocracy was acknowledged by local sedentary agriculturalists, and Herodotus mentions "Scythian ploughmen . . . who sow corn . . . for selling" - they may have been proto-Slavs.

What of hierarchical systems? They are of a piece with kinship and gender systems; that's integral to the premise of this study. For the nomads, it is very clear-cut: the military demands of aggressive nomadic society required a robust dominance hierarchy, and that carried over into strongly patrilineal kinship systems and male-dominance in gender relations.

Oddly enough, the Greeks thought, quite mistakenly it appears, that the Scythians were matriarchal. They may have been confusing them with the Sarmatians, for Sarmatian girls were trained and initiated as warriors before taking up their domestic duties, even though the fact that they then took up domestic duties as subordinates shows that it could not have been a matriarchal society as such. Also, the Greeks may have been reading a great deal into Herodotus' story of the Scythian wives who raised a breed of opponents in the face of their husbands' 28 year absence. But it is precisely stories like this one that reveal, in my opinion, a more complex pattern of corporate gender relations during the Slavic ethnogenetic moment. Furthermore, the Greeks may have been unconsciously trying to tone down Scythian machismo by subjecting the warlike herders to a feminizing influence. Group minds do this sort of thing.

What of hierarchical kinship and gender systems in the ancestral Slavic communities? Well, that is the "X" of this study. We don't know much about such systems. Sedentary horticulturalists didn't get around much, so contemporary historians left only sketchy descriptions of them. Since writing systems for Slavic weren't to be invented for some time yet, there are no linguistic artifacts as such in the digs for this period, except for a few place names. But taking the data we do have from history, linguistics, and archaeology that is related to this topic, we can use the logic of evolutionary psychology, and sometimes even data from literary works, to define coordinates and plot lines of convergence, not unlike the way astronomers determine the existence of previously unknown stars by observing the perturbations in the visibly known stars.

As noted above, Herodotus passes along a story about Scythian women who, during their husbands' 28-year absence on a campaign against the Persians, mated with their slaves to raise a generation of young warriors. When the older generation of males returned, the young men fought them, but were defeated and re-enslaved. While it would be a mistake to read this description of events at face value, we may learn some valuable things from the story. It suggests a pattern of corporate gender behavior that is fully consonant with what we know of foraging societies, where men hunt and women gather. It is probably accurate to think of military groups as evolving out of hunting groups, and given long absences, such behavior is plausible. What is interesting is that the women, the young men, the slaves, and the older men behave as "sodalities" (status groups) within the larger ethnos, defending their interests against other sodalities. In fact there are genetic differences between these gender sodalities that make them in some respects different *ethnoi*. Given the virtual certainty that such military groups sowed some wild oats on bivouac, the men participated genetically in other ethnicities. Likewise the women's corporate act may be seen as a counter move in sociobiological terms.

Some early passages of the Russian 'Primary Chronicle' (*Tale of Bygone Years – Povest' vremennykh let*) suggest such corporate gender behavior at Spring fertility festivals, attributed to 'Amazons':

"Once a year, near the Spring days, they leave their land and copulate with the local men, considering this time to be a certain solemnity and a great holiday. When they conceive in the womb, they again flee away from those places." To be sure, this text was written much later and its ethnographic section, quoting religious sources, had a primary interest in condemning promiscuity, so it would be a mistake to take its information at face value. But the corporate genetic decisions it describes are fully consonant with the sociobiological niches of the immediately post-foraging world.

The farmer/cowman dyad likewise reflects sociobiological dichotomies. As incipient systems, herding and horticulture may be linked first to hunting and gathering respectively, and at a deeper level they are linked with male and female sociobiological strategies. Aggressive nomadism capitalizes on reproductive strategies favoring male genetic fitness, such as multiple partners, short-term bonds, rape, and aggression among males, while sedentary horticulture uses a strategy favorable to females in sociobiological theory, to wit, long term nurturing of offspring. This is another echo of the androtypic and gynotypic behavioral templates. The symbiotic dyad of nomadic and sedentary societies during this period seems to be gender motivated, or at least gender linked.

# Gender and kinship in proto-Slavic grammar and life

Of course any discussion of corporate gender behavior brings us to linguistics. If you've ever studied a language that has grammatical gender, you know that it often has little to do with biological sexuality. (If your native language has grammatical gender, you probably don't think about it much, unless you are a linguist, because things our brains got used to before the age of 2 tend to remain subliminal in our unconscious minds.) We don't fully understand what these categories meant as language was evolving. It had something to do with sex, but wasn't completely coterminus with it - There are those confusing matters like the significant number of languages in which the word for "maiden" or "virgin" is neuter in grammatical gender, not to mention nonsexual words where gender assignment seems random and just silly. All of that is beyond this paper's scope, but there are a few details of the system of grammatical gender in Slavic that are significant for our topic.

Historical linguists agree that in Indo-European languages, feminine and masculine were subdivisions of the category "animate" ('living'), and in Common Slavic, animacy is still a declension category, but as a subdivision of "masculine". Since Common Slavic seems to have branched off from Indo-European by about 500 AD, it must have been precisely during the centuries of domination by androtypic nomads (Scyths, Sarmatians, Goths) that these grammatical categories took the peculiar shape they have in modern Slavic.

Feminine nouns and animate masculine nouns differ in an important way with regard to a category we may call "passability" - the capacity to be affected by other entities, denoted by the accusative case. (Readers unfamiliar with the concept of grammatical "case", for example native speakers of English who have not studied foreign languages, may think of the way the personal pronoun changes when it denotes the direct object: "him", "her", "them" instead of "he", "she", "they". This is the "case" that talks about being acted upon instead of being the performer of an act.) For males the category of passability (accusative) is conflated with that of possession; that is to say, masculine direct objects are denoted by a possessive ending ("genitive", denoting "of"),while for females the accusative case endings (denoting direct object) are distinct. For this reason, the feminine accusative ending seems the primary marker of passability, of the "acted upon" as opposed to the "actor". Thus for males the case system is less finely modulated than for females, and for men the category of passability ("acted upon") is linked, contradictorily, to an aspect of male power (possession). These features are quite what we would expect, given frequent male absence and incipient patriarchality.

Two exceptions must qualify this observation, both such as to confirm rather than undermine the hypothesis. First, in her core role, most central to the life of the community, the female is impassable: 'mother' (*mat'*) is the same in the naming case (nominative) and the case of passability (accusative, "acted upon" - Interestingly, so is 'daughter'. Second, in the archaic language, the males most important to the community, at all status levels, were denoted by words which had an ending we now would call feminine, a final '-a': 'big shot' (*vel'mozha*), 'chieftan' (*voevoda*), 'judge' (*sud'ya*), 'uncle' (*dyadya*), 'daddy' (*tyatya*), 'man' (*muzhchina*), 'servant' (*sluga*), 'slave' (*raba*) -- the modern versions of these words tend to keep their "feminine" endings but are used with masculine adjectives, masculine antecedents, and other masculine modifiers. To be sure, some of these denoted power roles (the first three), but the feminine ending lent them a certain vulnerability. This suggests a dichotomy of proximal vs. distant males - males in the immediate community as opposed to males further away, the latter more potent. This suggests a society with hyperactive patriarchal authority, to be sure, but in which male dominance was continually shaped, even subverted, by corporate feminine interests. Indeed, is this not the very signature element of the relationship between abusive leaders and submissive subjects in Slavic political systems during the historical period?

So what is known about kinship systems for proto-Slavs? All but one of the Indo-European kinship terms for the immediate family are preserved in Common Slavic, although they lose the '-er' suffix which had marked them as kinship terms in Indo-European (compare Slavic '*brat*', Germanic '*Bruder*', English '*brother*'; Slavic '*doc*', Germanic '*Tochter*', English '*daughter*'), and they are assigned to different declension categories as the Common Slavic gender system takes shape. So what is the missing family word? Which one disappeared?The linguistic evidence shows us that the Indo-European word for "father" or "patriarch" (related to Latin, *pater*, which is what this study will call it from here on) disappeared from Balto-Slavic sometime during this period to be replaced by a word denoting some kind of avuncular relationship, which later evolved into the Slavic word for "father". To be sure, the avuncular Indo-European word in question, *atta*, is well attested in Indo-European as an endearing term for father. Further, linguists are agreed that *pater* did not necessarily refer to the biological father of ego, but had a range of meaning relating to the social and even philosophical dimensions of the patriarchal role. Nonetheless, the disappearance of *pater* from Slavic language implies the disappearance of a class of persons from Slavic communities: powerful young males in the immediate community. The word must have disappeared because the type of person it denoted disappeared. I would suggest that several phenomena contributed to this disappearance. First, a good many young Slavic men went off to serve as mercenaries in the armies of neighboring civilizations. But that does not seem sufficient cause, and it begs the question of why they went.

# Genocide, rape, and the evolution of the family

Two genetic strategies of the warlike nomads of the area must have had a the effect of depleting the supply of young males as competent agents in proto-Slavic communities: males-only genocide and conquest rape.

Males-only genocide crops up with gruesome regularity in human communities, although we always seem oddly surprised by it. Its recent outbreaks in south Slavic territory lends credence to the idea that it may have been a feature of the ancestral environment, and the fact that it has been employed on all sides of an ethnic conflict suggests that it may be present as an incipient system, a predisposition favored by the physical and cultural environment in times of ethnic stress. In any case, historians tell us that Scythians typically killed or enslaved conquered locals, and that when a Scythian king pronounced a death sentence, all male relatives were killed. Archaeologists have noted the disappearance of proto-Slavic cultural materials (hill forts, small villages, certain burial practices) during the Gothic period (200-400 AD), and Latvian-American archaeologist Marija Gimbutas hazarded the comment: "It is unthinkable that the north-western invaders would have exterminated local inhabitants on their arrival". Odd that someone who hailed from central Europe in the 20th century would have found such a thing unthinkable. But perhaps our best example of males-only genocide during the proto-Slavic ancestral period is a story (from Roman historian Jordanes, of Gothic origin, writing in Byzantium) of the slaughter, in 375, of the Antic King Boz with all of his sons and 70 of his leading male citizens ("*et*

*LXX primatibus*") by the Ostrogothic king Vinitar after his defeat at the hands of the new invaders, the Huns. These practices were very likely not ethnically specific; very likely they were practiced by all of the warlike groups in the area during this period. Likewise it matters little whether Dvornik and Gimbutas are correct in seeing the Antes ruled by Boz as a proto-Slavic group. The role of perpetrator or victim is one prescribed by the position of a community in the bipolar tension beween "farmers and cowmen." Males-only genocide, like its concomitant, conquest rape, becomes a cultural choice available to any ethnic group selecting the aggressive strategy in this bipolar dyad. Incipient systems of this type seem to operate as toggle switches.

Conquest rape, alas, appears to be a universal concomitant of war, even in the

20th century. It is commonly claimed, especially by those justly decrying its horrible ubiquity, that it is 'unnatural'. This is an odd claim; what could be meant by an aberrant behavior which is universally distributed? Obviously that it is abhorrent, and this study certainly agrees that conquest rape is abhorrent.

Describing it as an 'incipient system' may help us out of this quagmire. Its undeniable ubiquity shows us that it is a behavior that can be supported by human male neurophysiology. It is equally clear that cultural systems can and do restrain it to varying degrees, but under certain types of stress, when those cultural constraints weaken, it can break out anew in all its ugliness. It doesn't really help to say that it is absent from the wiring until taught by groups of patriarchal males (the standard claim of the "politically correct" left), since the origin of such patriarchal culture is no easier to explain than is conquest rape itself. One needs to go no further than the Bible so see that it has been and continues to be part of the repertoire of human behavior during wartime. How much more so it must have been, alas, in aggressively androtypic groups like the Scythians and other nomadic warriors of the Slavic ancestral period. The underground Soviet-era Russian anthropologist Lev Gumilyov explained the population explosion of the proto-Slavic "ethnogenetic moment" thus: "...they weren't particularly shy about relations with conquered women, while [the women] loved the . . . children and nurtured them in their own language, to gain them entrance to a high status in their own tribes." What is needed for a population explosion, Gumilyov argued, is not many men but a lot of conquered women.

That conquest rape has the status of a genetic strategy became gruesomely clear in some of its recent outbreaks. In some of the Yugoslav rape camps of the 1990s, women who conceived were given special privileges and care until they gave birth. But at the same time, this underlines the subrational character of the behavior, for the 'strategy' was not thought out consistently - there was no suggestion that offspring of such rapes could be anything but borderline, low-status members of their fathers' ethnic groups. And just as often there would be no concern for the lives or offspring of the impregnated victims. Simple humiliation of the enemy has been closer to the conscious surface for this behavior. Further, it disables enemy reproductive systems rather than acting as a reproductive positive for the rapists' group.

During the Slavic ancestral period, such conquest rape not only rendered paternity uncertain in proto-Slavic communities, but created a porous genetic boundary between androtypic nomads and gynotypic horticulturalists, complicating the character of ethnicity. Of course the nomads had wives too, but they were typically left behind during campaigns. Genetically speaking they wouldn't have been much different from groups their husbands plundered, although there would have been tremendous social, economic and political differences.

The other factor contributing to the lowered status of young married males in ancestral Slavdom was no doubt the practice of snokhachestvo. It is well attested in ancestral Slavic communities that a powerful elder male (a patriarch, but here called "granddad", not 'pater', could demand a sort of droit de seigneur with his daughters-in-law, thus demoting his sons from their roles as biological fathers and as competent members of the community. Such behaviors were facilitated by the character of the proto-Slavic family as a "big family" (an extended nuclear family), dominated by a grandfatherly figure.

The resulting pattern is clear: power (sexual, military, and social) is held by distal males, warlike bands of rapists speaking other languages, or by local elders who are distal in a generational sense ("granddads"). Young males in the immediate community are powerless. They are either slaughtered by the foreign soldiers who rape their wives, or robbed of their sexual rights to their women by their own fathers. Small wonder many of those who were left chose to spend their lives fighting in armies for Marcus Aurelius, Justinian, or even Atila. Those who stayed at home were no doubt reduced to very peripheral roles indeed, in their families and in their communities. Small wonder babbling children started calling them by a derivative from the word for 'uncle/aunt', a word which later evolved into the Slavic word for "father".

Proto-Slavic may have had a classificatory system of kinship terminology which used one term for all immediate ancestral kin one generation removed, excluding the mother. In Proto-Indo-European, family words sometimes signified members of kin groups rather than specific relationships - There were traces of an "avuncular system" (an 'uncle' system). A practical acknowledgment of *snokhachestvo* may have resulted in the inclusion of the grandfather in this class. This strongly suggests that Slavic kinship passed through an avuncular stage, most likely on the mother's side. If we assume "aunt" and "uncle" to be the maternal variety, then "father" is the member of the immediate family group with the lowest level of certainty of genetic relatedness to the offspring of "mother", especially in view of nomadic conquest rape. Also, given the probability that maternal cross-cousin marriage was practiced among proto-Slavs, the roles of father-in-law and maternal uncle converge. "Uncle" (maternal), a word derived from "grandfather", is thought to be a local expression of a ethnological universal. Such generalized kin-terms could have referred to maternal uncle and aunt, grandfather, father, and finally father's siblings. The bifurcation of the term to refer to more specific kin may have taken place after this, after the avuncular term was applied to all of these members of the 'avuncular class,' but before the historic period of common Slavic. Indeed the Slavic kinship system could have passed through a generational stage to a bifurcate merging stage before finally proceeding to a (patri-)lineal one.

How must such a change have affected the patriarchal character of the proto-Slavic family and the patrilocal character of Slavic marriage practices? Indo-European families were patriarchal (witness the range of meaning covered by pater) and their post-marital residence pattern was patrilocal (the bride goes to live with her husband's family) - witness the fact that Proto-Indo-European language had words for the wife's ancestral inlaws (her father's parents), , but none for the husband's (words for which, in modern Russian, are Slavic coinages, most likely from the avuncular root!) Contemporary Russian families are also patriarchal and patrilocal. Would the changes in kin terms suggested above (the disappearance of the father) indicate a temporary shift in this pattern? Does this mean that Soviet anthropologists and some others were correct in assuming that ancestral culture was matriarchal, or at least matrilocal? I suspect that this may be so in myth, but was very likely not the case in actuality; many anthropologists are skeptical. An interesting intermediate possibility is the "matrifocal family", which combines "an expectation of strong male dominance in the marital relationship and as head of the household, coupled with a reality in which mother-child relations are solidary and groups of women, daughters and daughters' children emerge to provide a basis of continuity and security." Sociologist Raymond Smith argues that "we can find 'matrifocality' in domestic relations in a wide range of situations, from those where males virtually monopolise political, economic, and ritual life . . . to those where women are active . . . in those spheres . . . ." Perhaps such matrifocality could have been characteristic of the proto-Slavic communities.

# Family Shape in Russian Folktales

The great Russian folkorist Vladimir Propp, in his landmark study, *The Morphology of the Folktale*, pointed out that virtually all folk stories tell the same tale. His examples are all Russian, but the underlying pattern he found works for "Puss 'n Boots", "St. George and the Dragon", *Star Wars*, and indeed just about anything that can be called folklore. The young hero is forced to leave his home due to some awful misfortune, he travels to a foreign land where he encounters a love interest and an enemy, he kills the enemy and marries the girl, replacing her father as king in her land. From our point of view, with an interest in understanding the family structures that result from the dramatization of violence, it is clear that this lovely fairy tale could be a mythic retelling of conquest rape by violent nomads.

Propp's "Morphology" is the only place where matrilocal residence practices (groom moves to bride's home) actually show up in Slavic ethnic materials. The paradigm outlined in Propp's questing myth is one of matrilocal exogamy by conquest: the legendary hero leaves his homeland and becomes king in his bride's land, after conquering mythical enemies he finds on the way. In other words, the male marries into the female's family, but his move involves violence, and once he gets there he takes over. Propp's Slavic folk tale may provide a mythic account of conquest and rape.

If the matrilocal pattern reflected in the questing tale is a response to repeated conquest rape and subsequent assimilation rather than a reflection of an actual stage during which matrilocality was practiced, the paradigm raises important questions about the manner in which oral literature records historical reality. Perhaps it partially answers them as well. Folklore is not ethnography, but a product of the cultural systems ethnographers write about. The information it gives us about the history of the culture is not literal but symbolic. Symbolically or mythically, the folktale may reflect an archaic behavior, a wished for behavior, or a pivotal moment of change in behavior. But the construction of such a legend is a collective "believed-in imagining", and the line between fiction and fact is non-existent for the participants.

Actual Russian marriage customs involve patrilocal exogamy: the bride leaves her home to take up a very low-status position in her husband's household. This disjunction between folkore and folk practice must arise through one of the above three modes of symbolic representation. Perhaps turning the the conquering rapist-progenitor into a questing prince, a literary hero, tames him in theory, while his eventual sedentarization through the adoption of horticulture tames him in actuality. Some of the nomads of the area (with the striking exception of the last group, the Mongols) remained in the area after conquest, modifying or abandoning their nomadic and aggressive ways. Indeed, the early centuries of the historic period in Slavic territory were roughly coterminus with the twilight of aggressive nomadism (again, with the exception of its last great outbreak, the Mongols). Propp himself links the epos with the shift from an ancestral family type to monogamy.

Ironically, however, it has typically been the culture of the overrun groups that has survived intact and set the tone of the resulting hybrid culture (an example is the Vikings who founded Kiev, then stayed, began speaking east-Slavic, and became princes of "Rus" - a term they may have brought with them). Conquerors assimilate down, while subject cultures marry up (something anthropologists call "hypergamy"). Such assimilation must have happened countless times in post-neolithic eastern Europe, although the folk tale dramatizes it as a single event: the hero leaves his home land and attains the princess' hand in his chosen country after doing battle, and finally sets himself up as king in her land.

## Bye-Bye, Daddy

The traumas caused by a millenium of conquest could have been sufficient to expunge the word pater from the lexicon of kinship. The collective memory could be a constructed one, perhaps based on a number of near instances, or perhaps based merely on prevalent attitudes which necessitated a constructed myth or "believed-in imagining".

Or possibly the actual disappearance of fathers, perhaps under extremely stressful circumstances, and an extended period of absence, produced this turn-around in this central lexical feature. Several instances of males-only genocide, comparable to what the 1990s saw in the south Slavic lands, could have effected the change.

We can think of events that have left deep and thorough impressions on the ethnic consciousness: the '91 putsch, the October revolution, the death of Stalin. Couldn't the crucifixion of Antic King Boz with his sons and 70 of his foremost retainers have left such a "flash-bulb memory" in the minds of those men's wives and children? Perhaps they constituted virtually the whole population of a community of speakers of proto-Slavic. If Boz' group was a localized "big man society," 70 men could have represented the bulk of the male population - such societies range in size from 100 to 500. On the other hand, if it was a chiefdom, population would have been larger. Jordanes of course calls Boz a "king" ('rex'), but after all, modern anthropological distinctions were not available to him.

Certainly papa disappeared at this moment, rather dramatically. Surely the episode Jordanes records was not the only time this happened. How many times? In what communities, of what size? How closely spaced? Lasting how long? We don't have specific answers to these questions, but the linguistic evidence, and the survival of males-only genocide as an incipient system in modern populations, all suggest that it was very likely not an isolated incident. Who would have been left, besides the mothers and children? A class of older generation kin. Let's call them all "uncle."

# Gynotypic and Androtypic Paradigms: Incipient Neurocultural Systems

I have been using the term 'incipient system' to describe a number of the behaviors I have been discussing. It now behooves me to explain what I mean, and that will require a digression in a very different direction, toward the discussion of the mechanics of what may be called 'neurocultural' evolution.

Well, the genome map is out now and, wonder of wonders, it does not answer all of our questions. Genes, after all, only produce amino acids, and the 'behaviors' effected by those substances often seem trivial to the cultural historian; they are microscopic, they are nano-behaviors. Now I do not even begin to have the expertise to speak with authority about the genome itself. But as a scholar who

studies patterns, I can comment on
some of the patterns that are emerging
from the earliest writing on the new, now
'completed' genome map. Scientists are
talking about hierarchies of genes, about
the lateral interface between genes,
about pathways and rankings of genes.
At the level of behaviors we can actually
look at, such interfacing pathways or
systems are apparently as important as
the genes themselves. And it seems is
quite clear that such systems of
interfacing genes can be affected by the
environment, including the cultural
environment. A gene may not be
acquired or culturally transmitted, but a
culture or an environment may inculcate
or reinforce a pathway or linkage. If the
environment can activate or turn on a
particular incipient behavioral system, it
seems clear that the culture can learn to
imitate the environment in this regard.
This opens up a vast expanse of territory

between nature and nurture with elements of both, inseparable from either. At this early stage of exploring this territory it is impossible for us to make conclusions about it. But our speculations can open doors for further research; if we speculate with care and insight, the scientific results down the road could be prodigious.

One highly interesting aspect of recent work in genetics is the discovery that genetic competition occurs on the chromosomal level, and is gender dimorphic. That is to say that x- and y-chromosomes compete in human development. This is an outgrowth of the 'selfish gene' theory of Richard Dawkins, and experimental work based on it. Dawkins put forward that the 'optimon' or beneficiary of change in evolution, and thus the driving force behind natural selection, was not the individual, certainly not the species, but simply the gene striving to reproduce itself at the expense of its fellows. This has opened the door to a whole experimental field called ICE (for "interlocus contest evolution"), in which the competing interests of x- and y-chromosomes are seen as pitted against each other. I am not sure whether it is more appropriate to see this as a pair of struggling opponents (the view usually taken by geneticists I've read) or as a symbiotic dyad, but in any case the significance of the metaphor for the present study is overwhelming. It is possible to characterize gender typologies at the microscopic level as well as at the level of individuals. That metaphor suggests a potential validation of the methodology used here, in which gender typical behavior is seen as operating at the group level. I can't help but think of a set of nesting dolls (matryoshki , and, I guess, patryoshki), where the same features are seen writ large, medium, and small.

So how does a neurocultural trait evolve. A few basic principles are becoming clear anyway. Several elements create the physical brain: genetic inheritance, physical environment during critical developmental periods, and cultural environment, which becomes more reflexive and rich in previously construed meanings with every generation. In homo sapiens, which evolves culturally as well as genetically, neurophysiology (built thus by the genome and the environment together) becomes an 'internal environment,' a set of givens in the context of which the evolving entity selects, retains, or suppresses behavioral traits to serve its needs. Since the culturally evolving entity is a group of minds, the rules and priorities constraining selection change; the needs are to some extent self-defined (sometimes even consciously). The whole process becomes faster, more flexible, and less risky, but like natural selection, it selects traits as adaptations to external and internal environment. Cultural construction becomes an adaptive tool as we 'write' cultural software to make sense of our physiology and environment.

The genome, behavior, and environment act as a closed loop with no single control center. It is impossible to say that either the genome or the environment determines behavior wholly. Behavior is always produced by an interaction, and culture becomes a part of this loop. When culture involves choices by beings who believe themselves to be free, and when those 'free' choices occur against a randomized [virtually, at least, even if not actually] field of options, then one can take the quote marks off - free human choice becomes part of the loop that determines behavior. Yet this does not diminish our ability to analyze behavior as the product of the interactions of environment, genome, and culture. Although Dostoevsky's "underground man" would be surprised to learn of it, we can have behavioral science and freedom too.

Geographical and historical specifics thus shape the ethnos' construction of its givens, and also become part of the givens to be construed. Likewise, inherited (neuro-)physiology shapes constructions of our world, but is itself construed as part of our world. Eventually, extant details of culture become part of the shaping environment as well as part of the trait set being shaped. In this process, a trait may lose its tether to its genetic function, although not its genetic etiology; homo sapiens remains a biological creature. But as it is used by the ethnos in cultural selection, a trait may float free as a building block in whatever the evolving ethnos is creating. (Example: status hierarchy in a monastery exists because it enhanced reproductive fitness of ancestors, but the celibate group uses it for proximate goals, ignoring genetics.)

Cultural selection has the elements of natural selection: variation, randomness, selection, biased environments, and differential survival of products. But it may ignore genetic evolution, as the ethnos, or group mind, defines its needs with no regard to genetics, even while the genome, which produces the individual minds that comprise it, continues to evolve genetically. This gives the ethnos a fine-tuning knob on evolution, enabling us to respond rapidly and sensitively to environmental needs, and with low risk. Thus the group mind or ethnos becomes the 'optimon' or beneficiary, to use Dawkins' term, of cultural evolution, just as Dawkins' 'selfish gene' is the optimon of genetic evolution. Of course one must remember that the ethnos does not always define its adaptive needs consciously, and not always wisely.

In this context, gender typical group behavior can operate as what I call an 'incipient system,' a concept which can help us cross the minefield between nature and nurture. Although a cultural proclivity may not be hard-wired by the genome, neurophysiology enables a range of cultural possibilities. Along with the physical environment it may favor some of them. These are incipient systems " the neurological 'hardware' that is available for various cultural 'software' applications. It becomes appropriate to talk about a 'neurocultural template.' Incipient systems are privileged neural circuits, if you will, privileged by experiences in the physical and cultural environment. They are enabled by the genome but selected by the organism or group as cultural novelties are developed, adopted, and selectively retained in response to the needs of the physical and cultural environment. These needs are defined by the ethnos itself, usually unconsciously, sometimes consciously. They display a complex relation of genome to cerebral cortex (by contrast with behaviors dictated by the genome [e.g., exogamy] and with those preserved wholly in the cortex [e.g., lacemaking]). Such neuroculturally determined behaviors must arise and become entrenched with long term environmental (historical) regularities, and may often be dormant for long periods, seeming weaker than cortical patterns, only to show up again under stress or when activated by some other trigger in the physical or cultural environment.

## The Paradigm in Modern Russian Society

Let me refine my hypothesis: gender-typical action paradigms in Slavic culture are linked to, and partly generated by, an ancestral kinship paradigm in which fathers are either tyrannical or absent. Their absence can create something of an executive vacuum, which can be filled only by individuals who are distant, either physically or (more often) socially.

When indigenous authority systems finally do arise, they are hypertrophic, disfunctionally patriarchal, attacking rather than administering the polity. This political response to the perceived power deficit is 'androtypic.' Since the pattern originates in the kinship system as a gender trait, particularly as impaired male behavior, this behavioral template relates to the old cliche about Russia's feminine soul. The female behavioral correlate to this impairment template, although it is also dysfunctional, is an accommodation or adaptation to the ancestral circumstances that produced the impairment. And it gives its signature to the culture. The cultural response to the androtypic political formation is a 'gynotypic' paradigm, which allows itself to be co-opted by hypertrophic authority, but seeks to subvert it rather than taking direct action.

The pattern exists at many levels, including individual, family, and the polity as a whole. Similar patterns have been put forward in some sociological writing on the Soviet period. One sociologist describes a Russian family type comprising a motherly wife and the husband who acts liker her child. The female is dominant but both accept the ideology of patriarchy, even to the point of her putting up with beatings and pretending to be more affected than she is - The pattern has been around a long time. A recent variation is a more recent Soviet women's type, a woman who accepts professional responsibilities outside the home but submits to patriarchy within it. Then there is also the "nothing man," who has been deflated by the trends of recent history and is alcoholic and passive; he has lost his sense of maleness. One tends to see the causes of such paradigms in recent history, but they may actually stretch back to a much earlier period.

Indeed, the stereotype of the stymied Russian intellectual, unable to take significant action, is a stock character in Russian literature (as in life), from the superfluous men of 19th century fiction to the peripatetic drunks of the era of stagnation. Indeed the very existence of the 'era of stagnation' as a cultural period stands witness to this truism. Comments about Russia as sufferer, about its passivity or even masochism, about its reliance on foreign models for personal and national identity, all relate to this behavioral set.

What about the empowerment of women? We have not seen, until recently anyway, many formalized institutions for female executive roles (except behind the scenes and, charismatically, in informal social settings) either in Dostoevsky's fiction or in Slavic culture, ancestral or contemporary. The reasons for this irrational and dysfunctional exclusion (which is of course not unique to Slavic culture, but perhaps more than usually prevalent in it) lie partly in the kinship structures under investigation here.

# Back to Fyodor Mikhailovich

But these are golden dreams! We need to have another look at the literary work that occasioned the hypothesis. We have observed a pattern of alternation between abusive fathers and absent ones, and we have looked at some linguistic, sociological, and historical materials that might account for this behavioral dichotomy. Essentially what we are looking at is a typology of powerful distal males and powerless proximal ones. Is this what we observe when we return to Dostoevsky's fiction? Just so.

Let us look first at Dostoevskian fathers. It is well-nigh impossible to think of a Dostoevskian father who plays a major positive role in his children's lives. Those who try are either pathetic (Pokrovsky in *Poor Folk*, Snegiryov in *The Brothers Karamazov* ) or ridiculous (Verkhovensky *pere* in *The Devils* ). Fathers who do play an active role tend either to sell their daughters (Marmeladov in *Crime and Punishment*, Epanchin in *The Idiot* ) or tyrannize over their sons (Versilov in *A Raw Youth*, Fyodor Karamazov). But in most of Dostoevsky's fictions, fathers are simply absent altogether or they are cardboard cutout figures with no role at all to play in the action.

In Dostoevsky's fiction we frequently find a triangle comprising a proximal powerless male, a distressed female, and a distal powerful male. This is paradigmaticaly related to the 'rescue triangles' I have discussed elsewhere, but not coterminus with them, as the proximal male seldom attempts, and even less often effects, rescue (but note Ordynov's rescue, in "The Landlady"). Of course one may ask, proximal to whom? Usually to ego, that is, to the character the narrator or reader is most likely to identify with; in the early fiction usually the young Petersburg dreamer, like Ordynov; later a series of characters clearly derived from that prototype. In the triangle Shatov-Shatova-Stavrogin (*The Devils*), we have a rather precise rendition of the pattern outlined above for ancestral Slavic communities: a local 'father' shelters his wife and her child begotten by an absent, powerful male. In the triangle Dmitri-Grushenka-Fyodor Pavlovich (*The Brothers Karamazov*), the pattern is closer to that suggested by *snokhachestvo*.

Note the marital arrangements implicit in the aesthetically unsuccessful novels The *Eternal Husband* and *A Raw Youth*, where low status males (Trusotsky, Makar Dolgoruky) raise children sired on their putative wives by high status mobile males (Vel'chaninov, Versilov).

The marital system is once again the one we have discovered in Slavic pre-history. But the biological fathers move closer to real parenthood in the course of these works. Could it be that these works dramatize for us the evolutionary moment when the option of sedentary marriage became preferable to abusive nomadism? This could account for the dynamism of these salient issues, but also for the artistic failure of these works. In the final analysis the issue might just have been too explosive for a work of narrative fiction.

It is not hard to find examples of this paradigm in the work of other writers and in Russian culture generally: the Oedipal triangle of Turgenev's *First Love*, Treplyov-Nina-Trigorin in Chekhov's *The Seagull*, even Bezukhov-Natasha Rostova-Bolkonsky in some sections of Tolstoy's *War and Peace*. The opening pages of Tolstoy's "Father Sergius" reflect a similar situation vis-a-vis the tsar'. The point is that the localized male ego is emasculated by a variety of distant forces beyond his control. Indeed, the pattern could be said to underline the influential paradigm of "the superfluous man" in Russian literature.

The female fares no better. But her paradigm is different: she is abused and co-opted rather than being killed or driven off. Although her choices are limited, she may feel more control over her local environment than the male, but she can only exercise it in informal ways, by subverting the system. And it is her behavior paradigm that becomes definitive for Russian culture: at the local level, there is a sense that control may only be achieved by subversion, not by direct action.

This is the way in which Russian culture

is gynotypic or feminine. Note what the monk Silvestr advises his protege Anfim in the sixteenth century 'Household Rule'; he is waxing nostalgic about Anfim's mother and her high status in the community, then he adds this telling directive: "...be zealous in the same and behave thus; take upon yourself every kind of injury and endure...". The idea of Russian culture as feminine is an oft repeated observation, fleshed out most recently by Joanna Hubbs, who notes the replacement of feminine deities by masculine ones as herders came to power in the steppe. Here we see some actual socio-cultural mechanisms embodying such gynotypicality.

Psychologist Stephen Johnson, speaking about character development in individuals who in childhood faced stresses like paternal abandonment, outlines a paradigm that seems potentially valid for groups as well (see the matryoshka concept noted above): "extremely fundamental issues are faced early on in life, and . . . some early attempts at resolving them are based both on limited equipment and limited experience . . . . When the issues are faced in trauma, their early resolutions tend to become rigid and resistant to change. In this view these early solutions were often quite adaptive given the limitations of the environment and the limitations of the individual's capacities, but they often achieved an imperfect escape from them". Taken in a collective sense, this passage could be taken as a valid description of proto-Slavic adaptation to the disappearance of fathers. The personality features Johnson lists for the "abandoned child" coincide with some of the most common generalizations about Slavic character, lending credence to the idea that absent fathers could have been an important traumatic feature of Slavic ethnogenesis. These include weak assertiveness, self-directed aggression, resistance to change, and a tendency to "borrow identity".

# Conclusion

Now I must clarify one more time the way in which I see this happenning, in order to avert several 'incipient misunderstandings" of my theory. I am not saying that this paradigm is genetically hard wired, nor that such behavior paradigms occur only in Slavic culture, or that the behavior is universally found in all Slavs. Rather, I am suggesting that as an 'incipient system' this paradigm exists as a potential in all communities of homo sapiens brains; the hardware can support the software. In ancestral Slavic communities gynotypicality as an incipient system was favored by the physical, and eventually, the cultural environment; it became a (cultural) evolutionary niche, in bipolar symbiosis with its opposite. After a couple of dozen generations, it became part of the cultural environment, unconsciously entrenched in the cerebral cortices of all individuals of the community. It is entrenched as an option, but not necessarily expressed in all individuals or all situations. Although the information that is copied when it is transmitted is stored not by the genome but by the cerebral cortex, its entrenchment is still very deep. It could only be erased by bringing up individuals in isolation from others who share it. But if you did that they wouldn't be members of the ethnos any longer, never mind genetics. As noted earlier, patterns like this may be deeply embedded in the culture, even if they are not stipulated by the genome. What they amount to is an entrenched preference for a particular incipient system, which may lie dormant in non-stressful environments, but which may be triggered under stress. The stressed group identity cathexis we call nationalism may work in this way [e.g., recent Yugoslav history]. During the recent past in Russia, the stresses of the attempted transition to a liberal economy and a democratic political system have triggered the reassembly of some of the most dysfunctional aspects of earlier systems, the bifurcation of the political economy into an oligarchy and a dispossessed and disaffected mass, and the resulting impairment of confidence in one's own action potential among members of that mass. Hopefully it will also trigger the positive aspects of that dyadic paradigm, the gynotypic subversion of the abusive political and economic status quo through brilliant works of literature and culture.

*Bibliography and footnotes are available in the scholarly version of this study, published in The New Zealand Slavonic Journal in 2001, or online at www.voxdanubia.com/newfemsoul.html*